The Eastern Enlargement of the European Union

Nicholas Hopkinson

December 1994

Wilton Park Paper 91

Report based on Wilton Park Conference WPS 94/6: 12–16 September 1994: The European Union and Central Europe: From Association To Membership? in Association with the Council of Ministers, Warsaw at Natolin, near Warsaw.

London: HMSO

ISBN 0 11 701877 5
ISSN 0953–8542

Published by HMSO and available from:

HMSO Publications Centre
(Mail, fax and telephone orders only)
PO Box 276, London, SW8 5DT
Telephone orders 0171-873 9090
General enquiries 0171-873 0011
(queuing system in operation for both numbers)
Fax orders 0171-873 8200

HMSO Bookshops
49 High Holborn, London, WC1V 6HB
(counter service only)
0171-873 0011 Fax 0171-831 1326
68–69 Bull Street, Birmingham, B4 6AD
0121-236 9696 Fax 0121-236 9699
33 Wine Street, Bristol, BS1 2BQ
0117 9264306 Fax 0117 9294515
9–21 Princess Street, Manchester, M60 8AS
0161-834 7201 Fax 0161-833 0634
16 Arthur Street, Belfast, BT1 4GD
01232 238451 Fax 01232 235401
71 Lothian Road, Edinburgh, EH3 9AZ
0131-228 4181 Fax 0131-229 2734

HMSO's Accredited Agents
(see Yellow Pages)

and through good booksellers

CONTENTS

1 Introduction

Perhaps unthinkable in the Communist era, the accession of the six Central and Eastern European Countries (CEECs) is no longer a question of 'if' but 'when' and 'how' they will join the European Union (EU). In early 1994, the nature of CEEC and EFTA applicants for EU membership were quite different. The four EFTA applicants (Austria, Finland, Norway, and Sweden) were well qualified to join but many of their citizens appeared reluctant to join the EU. The CEECs do not yet qualify for membership but their governments and people were eager to join. The successful ratification of EU membership in Austria, Finland, and Sweden in late 1994 makes enlargement to the east all the more likely.

An accession negotiation is concerned with "the way in which an applicant country will function as a member ... (and) the relations between 'the future us'."[1] However, many still question whether the CEECs are capable of adopting, let alone adjusting to, the stringent requirements of EU membership. Although the establishment of democratic institutions in the CEECs has been completed, their proper functioning is far from complete. Similarly, the transformation into market economies has turned out to be much more difficult and costly than expected.

The key to accession for CEECs is to push market reforms forward rapidly. The market reforms have caused the CEECs to lose traditional markets in the former COMECON countries, and obliged them to re-orientate their trade towards the EU and EFTA. Yet bilateral Europe Association Agreements with the EU have only partly filled the vacuum. The continued successful adjustment of CEEC economies therefore relies on open markets in the EU, a predictable medium-term financial framework, free access to external financing, appropriate debt management policies, and an inflow of private capital and direct assistance.

---

[1] Graham Avery, *The European Union's Enlargement Negotiations*, The Oxford International Review (Summer Issue, 1994), p. 28.

Although the cost of 'non-Europe' has been calculated, no one has calculated the cost of 'half-Europe'. When assessing the two current and future CEEC applications for membership, the EU should not concentrate on their present economic situation but their economic potential and the bridging role that the CEECs can play between the EU and the former Soviet Union. Furthermore, the CEECs can help make the EU more competitive in the face of global competition from Japan and the United States by: expanding and securing markets; improving economies of scale in a larger European customs union; improving comparative advantage, particularly by offering cheaper wage labour; and improving competitiveness in areas where the EU economy itself is in the greatest need of restructuring (steel, textiles, basic chemicals and agriculture). Ultimately CEEC membership of the EU will require economic restructuring and reform within the EU itself.

From Europe Agreements to Essen

The recommendations and decisions adopted by the European Councils in Edinburgh, Copenhagen, Corfu and Essen indicate the growing will of the EU to engage in closer political and economic relations with the six CEEC associated states, as well as a growing EU interest to support efforts to ensure the convergence and integration of the CEECs with the EU.

By 1990, the EU had concluded 'second generation' treaties with all CEECs and the former Soviet Union. In December 1990, the EU opened negotiations on associate membership with the three, now four, Visegrad Group (V4) countries (the Czech Republic, Hungary, Poland and Slovakia). The Europe Agreements went beyond the 'second generation' agreements by establishing institutional frameworks for political dialogue and economic co-operation including aid and trade. Taking a longer view, the Europe Agreements were conceived as frameworks within which the CEECs can be prepared for accession.

Asymmetrical trade preferences are extended more rapidly to the associate states over a ten-year period. Certain 'sensitive' products are regulated by special protocols, notably textiles, coal and steel and agriculture. The Agreements aim to enable associate countries restructure their economies and make them more competitive. However, special protective clauses guarantee the protection of nascent industries and associate countries may take unilateral measures, such as raising duties, in order to protect them temporarily. In all sectors, except usually banking and insurance, associate member states will grant 'national treatment' for EU firms. The parties shall guarantee the repatriation of profits and capital connected with foreign investments for companies. Associate member states will strive to adjust their laws gradually to EU laws, one of the preconditions for gradual integration. Thus the Association agreements do not introduce fully the EU's four freedoms (free movement of goods, services, capital and people).

Each Europe Agreement also creates a Council of Association, which establishes within its own authority the rules of procedure regulating its activity, and has binding decision-making power in cases determined by the Treaties. The bilateral Councils are chaired alternately by the associate state concerned and the EU.

The multilateral framework with the V4 enhances dialogue by saving the time of the EU Presidency which would otherwise require more time-consuming individual discussions. Aided by a common history, similar economy and proximity, the V4 exchange views and co-operate closely amongst themselves. In addition to a free trade agreement and co-operation between the four defence ministries, the V4 submitted a joint memorandum entitled 'On strengthening Integration with the European Communities' to the EU Commission and Presidency in September 1992. However, the V4 remain free to act individually, a fact that has lead observers to remark that the V4 lost bargaining strength when negotiating the Europe Agreements.

In December 1992, the Commission's document "Toward Closer Association with the Central and East-European Countries" was submitted to the Edinburgh Council. It called on the Council to confirm its intention to accept the objectives of the V4 regarding future membership provided they complied with the necessary preconditions. The June 1993 Council in Copenhagen made, for the first time, eastern enlargement no longer a question of 'if' but only a question of 'how' and 'when'. The Council decided to admit the six associated CEEC countries that so desire provided that they are able to assume the obligations of membership: "Membership requires that the candidate country has achieved stability of institutions guaranteeing democracy, the rule of law, human rights and respect for and protection of minorities, the existence of a functioning market economy as well as the capacity to cope with competitive pressure and market forces within the Union. Membership presupposes the candidate's ability to take on the obligations of membership including adherence to the aims of political, economic and monetary union". A distinction was made between associated countries having Europe agreements and others.

The Copenhagen Council proposed that the associated countries enter into a structured relationship with the institutions of the Union within the framework of a reinforced and extended multilateral dialogue. It established a high level system of co-operation in matters falling within its authority including Trans-European Networks, energy, environmental protection, Common Foreign and Security Policy (CFSP) as well as co-operation in Justice and Home Affairs (JHA).

In order to have a functioning market economy, candidates must introduce market mechanisms and adopt the entire *acquis communautaire* (all EU legislation, regulations and customs). However, the economic conditions for membership are expressed in qualitative and not quantitative terms. In the case of Economic and Monetary Union (EMU), CEEC candidates are only required to 'adhere to its aims' rather than meet the convergence criteria.

The Copenhagen Council also noted that the Union's capacity to absorb new members and to maintain the momentum of integration are important considerations in deciding upon an eastern enlargement. Thus even if candidates fulfill the member-ship criteria, they can still be turned down if EU Member States conclude that the EU is unable, or unready, to absorb new members.

The Polish and Hungarian Association Agreements were the first to be ratified by all EU Member States. Accordingly, the governments of Hungary and Poland, believing that they made sufficient progress in meeting the preconditions for membership, submitted formal applications for membership to the Council in April 1994. The other four association agreements, with the Czech Republic, Slovakia, Bulgaria and Romania, have been recently ratified. Mandates for negotiating Europe Agreements with Estonia, Latvia and Lithuania have been agreed, and negotiations will start soon.

The Corfu Council in June 1994 asked the Commission to produce a report for the 9–10 December 1994 Essen Summit on the progress and strategy for preparing CEECs for accession. The Commission's paper "Europe and Beyond – A Strategy to Prepare the Countries of Central and Eastern Europe for Accession"aims to promote the integration of the associated countries by building on the basis of the Europe agreements. It also proposes that the same terms of the Association Agreements offered to the V4 should be extended to Romania and Bulgaria. Although the 1996 Inter-Governmental Conference (IGC) will precede eastern enlargement, negotiations on an eastern enlargement could commence as early as 1997. The Corfu communique does not stipulate whether the results of the 1996 IGC have to be ratified by Member States.

2   Member State Perspectives

Widening

Enlargement forces Member States to reconsider their objectives in the EU and redefine its future direction. Many Member State governments are reluctant to re-open a debate on the pace and scope of integration because they are still traumatised by the public reaction to the Maastricht Treaty. Governments are now convinced that any new plans for the future of the EU will have to gain legitimacy through public support, including referenda.

Member States vary in their enthusiasm and motivations for wanting to enlarge the EU eastwards. It is widely believed that the United Kingdom government enthusiastically espouses an eastern widening of the EU in order to slow or prevent the deepening of the integration process. British Prime Minister Major said in Warsaw on 1 August 1994 that the EU would not be complete until the CEECs were members and, at Leiden on 7 September 1994, he stated that a free, stable, prosperous and democratic Central Europe will be a huge benefit to the whole continent.

The United Kingdom Government believes it is hard to be precise about a timescale for membership. It is clear that accession negotiations will not begin until after the 1996 IGC, but how soon after that negotiations will commence depends on developments in both applicant countries and the EU. There can be no assumption that all the CEECs will join the EU at the same time because some candidates will be ready before others. Thus the emphasis must be on preparations and interim steps for accession. For example, the United Kingdom will continue to press for further liberalisation of trade, especially in agriculture.

By geography, history and culture, the Federal Republic of Germany has a special interest and obligation towards the CEECs, although it recognises that integration of the CEECs is a challenge for the whole of Europe. Germany wants to bring itself back into the centre of Europe and away from its edge. Four and a half decades of German post-war policy should be sufficient evidence to testify that it is not flirting with the earlier concept of 'schaukelpolitik' (seesaw policy) between East and West. Moving Germany back to the middle of Europe should benefit all Europeans.

Worried by instability in the east and potential mass migration from the east, Germany is pressing for an early eastern enlargement. The German Presidency submitted to the Essen Council a substantial strategy paper giving a clear and visible signal that the EU seriously wants to integrate the CEECs. It wants to develop a 'structured relationship' between the EU and CEECs as envisaged by the Copenhagen Summit. In practice, this means keeping a delicate balance between the necessary respect for the internal decision making process of the Union, and the necessary inclusion and possible participation of the CEECs. Secondly, it wants to improve the readiness and ability of CEECs to assume the *acquis communautaire*.

France and Spain now regard enlargement to the east as inevitable but they want assurances that an eastern enlargement will not weaken the EU or dilute it into a free trade area. Whilst welcoming the CEECs as part of 'our European family', France fears that the level of the EU's affluence and effectiveness may be adversely affected. As the new Member States are likely to have long transition periods, they should not be so long as to permanently stall the deepening of EU integration. France also remains reluctant to entertain any further reform of the CAP which will inevitably be raised as part of a CEEC negotiating agenda.

In spite of recent French accusations that Germany has put CEEC candidates' interests ahead of EU members, Member States have co-operated with the Commission in developing a 'pre-accession' strategy. The centrepiece of the strategy is a White Paper which in the Spring of 1995 will list measures for the CEECs to adopt in order for them to integrate themselves with the Single Market. The German foreign minister, Kinkel, said in late September 1994 that the White Paper should map out the road ahead for the CEEC's eventual integration: "One likely approach is for the Commission to draw up a list of between 100 and 150 measures for the CEECs to adopt in order to make their legislation compatible with EU standards. In return, the EU would phase out progressively anti-dumping measures and thereby expand the single European market eastwards".[2]

It is very difficult for applicants to undertake preparatory work for accession because points of view differ widely between and within the 12 EU Member States. It is not enough for CEEC

---

[2] David Buchan and Lionel Barber, *Road-map Sought for EU Applicants, Financial Times*, 21 September 1994.

applicants and potential applicants to work on proposals to integrate the CEECs that are often reduced to their lowest common denominator. CEECs want a clear road map to accession, and they want to negotiate on to the same basis for accession as Greece, Spain and Portugal.

Deepening

Recently old concepts like multi-track, multi-speed, Europe, Europe *à la carte*, two-tier Europe and a Europe of concentric circles have again been widely debated. Notably both the August 1994 Schauble paper proposed by Germany's CDU/CSU and the proposals by French Prime Minister Balladur have elaborated visions of a flexible Europe with an expanded membership to the East organised around an inner circle of fast-track countries.

The German and French approaches derive from a common philosophy: the pace and scope of European integration should not be dictated by the most reluctant members, or by those who cannot cope with the obligations of full membership. But there are also differences between them. While the CDU/CSU paper explicitly refers to a hard core of countries of the original six less Italy, the Balladur proposals do not envisage a central 'core' of the same countries pursuing faster integration in all fields. The French government therefore sees no reason why countries outside the final stage of EMU should not play a leading part in other fields like immigration or the CFSP.

The French and German proposals have forced the United Kingdom to clarify its views. Prime Minister Major has expressed preference for a multi-speed Europe in which some states should integrate more closely and quickly in certain areas than others. At Leiden he stated that "there is not, and never should be, an exclusive hard core either of countries or of policies". He does, however, believe that conformity by all members is right and necessary in international trade, the single market and the environment; in other policy areas, member states should be able to progress at different speeds. No Member State should be excluded from an area of policy in which it wants to and is qualified to participate.

3 Candidate and Other Perspectives

Lessons from the Finnish Application

Future enlargements will be entirely different from the 1993–4 EFTA enlargement because the circumstances, administrative structures, traditions, legislation, and material conditions vary from one candidate country to another. However, some lessons can be learned.

Finland, one of the four applicants for accession on 1 January 1995, presented its application after a fairly short but intensive domestic debate in March 1992. Negotiations began 1 February 1993 and agreement with the EU was reached in March 1994. In October 1994, the Finnish people voted to join the EU. In the history of successive enlargements of the EU, Finnish membership was gained in record time.

Efficient preparations, co-ordinated by the Ministry of Foreign Affairs, were essential for smooth progress in the negotiations. Preparations were required on the broadest range of issues in Finnish negotiating history, requiring the participation of more than 550 individuals from various ministries, other authorities, interest groups, social partners and political parties.

Finland's basic strategy in the negotiations was to concentrate on the most important issues, particularly agriculture and regional policy. However, this alone was not enough. When dealing with the EU, issues must be clearly spelt out and repeated time after time. Arguments have to be straightforward and simple. Finland realised towards the end of negotiations, to its dismay, that in some instances some of its most important key arguments were not familiar to the EU negotiating team.

In every phase of the negotiating process, timetables set have been met because there was a strong, gradually strengthening, political will. The material and technical preparedness of the EFTA applicants was accelerated thanks to the already close integration of EFTA countries with the EU, and the fact that the EU *acquis communautaire* had already been introduced by the European Economic Area (EEA) Agreement and individual national efforts since the late the 1980s. In any case, many aspects of the EEA, notably institutional arrangements, had to be renegotiated in the enlargement context.

Direct contacts with Member States and the Commission at the political and official level were carefully cultivated - this turned out to be a key success factor in the negotiations. Direct contacts between the applicant countries, although useful, were less significant than might have been expected. Although there was very close contact between the Nordic countries, each applicant had its own agenda to negotiate. The role of the EU Presidency was very important, and in the last phases of the negotiations, the active work of the troika became more and more important.

Finland did not encounter any major difficulties in the negotiations until the very last stages. In February and March 1994, the break-up of the negotiations was a real option, but ultimately it was avoided. Unexpectedly, the attitudes of certain Member States, hitherto believed to be positive, turned out to be less so. But the opposite also happened on some issues and in connection with other Member States. The concluding 'marathon' session was a demanding experience but, in spite of some alien methods, proved to be an efficient means of bringing the negotiations to a successful conclusion. However, after the conclusion of a final package, the parties have expressed varying interpretations of what had been agreed. This had a temporary effect on relations and had a temporary adverse impact on Finnish public opinion, which could have jeopardised the eventual positive referendum result.

Many issues not directly linked to the negotiations had an impact on the enlargement process. The negotiations, or at least their rapid progress, was threatened by a number of unrelated internal EU problems including: the Maastricht Treaty ratification difficulties in Member States, especially Denmark; attempts to link consent to enlargement with institutional reform; the blocking minority issues at the end of negotiations; and whether or not the European Parliament would vote on the Accession Treaty before its dissolution in mid-1994.

Finland regarded the result of the negotiations as satisfactory. Key objectives were reached with a few exceptions. For example, it is believed that special Nordic circumstances in agricultural support were not fully understood. Accordingly, the immediate alignment to EU agricultural prices will be difficult. Different interpretations of the results of negotiations on this issue added to domestic uncertainty and opposition.

Openness was an important aspect of Government policy during the negotiations. The Parliament was regularly kept up to date on progress and interest groups could take part in the formulation of negotiating positions. The media was briefed regularly and background information was given weekly.

The leading political party in the Government had the greatest difficulty in advocating membership, causing uncertainty about the governing coalition's commitment to membership. Ironically, the government's uncertain commitment actually encouraged growing public support for joining the EU because Finns traditionally do not like their governments to push too hard for a particular policy.

Before the Nordic referenda, Finnish public opinion was consistently more in favour of EU membership than that in Sweden and Norway. Public support for EU accession prevailed even though the Government's popularity was low and the economy was suffering from a dramatic drop in GDP. Finns voted to join partly due to historical factors and to anxiety about Finland's eastern neighbour, both factors not shared by the other EFTA candidates. An underlying feeling was that Finns regarded accession as an opportunity to join the EU and be accepted as a fully-fledged member of Western Europe, to which the vast majority of Finns have always believed they belonged. Many Finns were also attracted to the potential economic benefits of membership including lower consumer, mainly food, prices; a reduction of the high unemployment rate; more foreign direct investment; and lower yields on government bond prices. The positive result in the Finnish referendum encouraged Swedes to vote to join the EU but then Norwegians voted against membership for a second time.

The accession negotiations will be of great use when Finland starts participating in EU decision-making and procedures. The experience will help Finnish officials and politicians in defining Finland's role, to choose the correct procedures, and to establish national machinery to meet membership needs.

Poland

Poland, like other CEECs, has six basic options in its bid for membership: immediate full membership; full membership by 2000; membership in 2000 with transitional agreements; membership in 2007 with pre-accession and post- accession transitional arrangements; membership being postponed for an indefinite period, and the Europe Agreement not being fully implemented, thus blocking any progress on further integration. The first two and last two options are unrealistic and/or politically unacceptable for the CEECs.

The Polish public and all political parties are keen to join the EU. Poland has always been a part of Europe and therefore the Yalta division of Europe has never been accepted. Joining the EU would be considered as the real end to the division of Europe. Secondly, Poland is undergoing a rapid political, social and economic transformation, one that is difficult, costly and painful. Joining the EU serves as the clear-cut goal that enables the government and people to endure the transition.

Poland does not want to join a Europe à la carte which would accommodate many aspiring candidates, whatever their current political and economic situation. Poland wants to transform itself completely into a market economy in order to become a fully fledged EU member state. The 'Strategy for Poland', adopted by the Polish Parliament in mid-1994, outlines a medium term economic policy, based on: an open trading regime; sound macro-economic and structural adjustment policies; annual GDP growth targets of more than five percent, and 30 per cent total investment growth over the next three years. By skipping interim stages, Poland believes it will be able to adjust effectively and eventually meet world competition directly.

Poland has one of the fastest growing CEEC economies. Growth in 1993 was four per cent and is likely to be 4.5 per cent in 1994. Exports are growing rapidly, and are 20 per cent higher in the first half of 1994 compared with the same period in 1993. Unemployment has stabilised at around 16 per cent, lower than in Spain and just above the unemployment rate in Belgium. Half of Poland's debts to Western governments were written off in 1991, and in September 1994, the London Club of private creditors agreed to halve the value of Poland's commercial debt. With its external debt situation stabilised at acceptable levels, the Polish government and firms will again be able to access international capital markets.

By any measure, Poland is now a market economy. More than half of Poland's GDP is produced by the private sector, compared to between 40 to 65 per cent in most other CEECs (except 80 per cent in the Czech Republic) and Russia. Only five per cent of goods are subsidised or subject to government price controls. The Zloty is now fully convertible for businesses. A company can be formed without a government licence. Firms can sell where and what they want, and they can import and export freely. However, Poland's privatisation programme slowed in 1994 under the new government with disagreement over which state enterprises should be privatised. More than 5,000 firms remain state-owned.

Hungary

Hungary's Europe Agreement, signed in December 1991, is an essential step to membership. Under the Interim Agreement, trade and trade related issues have been applicable since March 1992. With the full entering into force of the Europe Agreement in February 1994, the Hungarian Government judged that Hungary was ready enough for it to submit the first CEEC application for EU membership in April 1994.

Accession to the EU has been the top Hungarian foreign policy priority since 1990. The Hungarian Government believes membership by 2000 is not too rapid a target even though the EU may perceive it to be. It hopes that negotiations on accession could start in 1997, culminating in an accession treaty that enters into force in 1999 or 2000. The Government recognises that future developments may change this timetable.

Mr. Laszlo Kovacs, the Foreign Minister, called on the Commission to draw up its own opinion on Hungary's application for membership before the 1996 IGC in order to speed up the process: "We want (applications) to be (considered) country by country. We are very much against the convoy principle".[3] Currently, all political parties support EU membership as well as a majority of public opinion. It is feared that if there is no clear timetable, then Hungarians will become disillusioned, and the perception will increase that Hungary is not wanted in the EU club.

The best policy to adopt in order to qualify for membership is the rapid transition to a market economy. More than half of Hungarian GDP is now generated by the private sector thanks to a major privatisation programme. The private sector is expected to grow in spite of a temporary slow-down in the privatisation programmme, attributable to the fact that the most attractive firms were privatised first. In order to complete the sale of the remaining state companies by 1998, in late 1994 the government approved sweeping changes to privatisation regulations.

---

[3] quoted in *Financial Times*, 23 November 1994

Without the target of EU membership by 2000, it will be difficult to convince foreign investors to continue to invest. Foreign direct investment (FDI) has been important in Hungary's economic transformation with $7.2 billion having flowed in since 1989, about half of all FDI flowing to the CEECs in the same period.

In its bid for early membership, Hungary has sought to implement the legal and institutional characteristics of a developed market economy. For example, an office of economic competition, the Stock Exchange, and a European-style banking and financial system have been established. Since 1988, a number of important laws and regulations have been adopted to approximate EU law, and the government has elaborated a medium and long term work plan to complete the approximation of EU laws.

In common with other CEECs, the liberalisation of trade has created rapidly rising deficits and the gravitation of trade towards the EU. Exports to the EU have grown from 25 per cent of all exports in 1989 to 47 per cent of all exports in 1993. Exports to the EU and EFTA combined constituted 60 per cent of all exports in 1993. Imports from the EU increased from 29 per cent of all imports in 1989 to 40 per cent of all imports in 1993 (58 per cent including EFTA countries).

Hungary's Europe Agreement makes some progress in the direction of a structured relationship. Hungary is ready to co-operate in the formulation and implementation of the CFSP, both on the basis of the provisions of the Europe Agreement on political dialogue, and in other frameworks such as the North Atlantic Treaty Organisation (NATO), Western European Union (WEU) and Partnership For Peace (PFP). As a first step in the participation of the CFSP, Hungary has appointed a shadow correspondent to join the European Corrrespondent System. In the multilateral dialogue between the EU and the Associated Countries, Hungary supports the elaboration of the 'pre-accession package' prepared by the EU Commission. Hungary is also ready to accept all the provisions concerning co-operation in the JHA pillar.

Romania and Bulgaria

The Government of Romania stated at the time of the signing of its Europe Association Agreement that its goal was to strengthen relations with the EU, leading towards its eventual full membership in the EU. The Europe Agreement recognises that accession to the EU is Romania's ultimate objective.

Security and prosperity are the key reasons for Romania and Bulgaria wanting to join the EU. Although Romania and Bulgaria recognise that each state should join at its own speed, depending upon individual circumstances, they want reassurance that all six associated CEECs will be treated in a similar, and undifferentiated, manner by the EU.

The details of the Romanian and Bulgarian Europe Agreements are somewhat different from the V4 agreements in their content. In order to bring the Romanian and Bulgarian Europe Agreements into line with the V4 agreements, an EU Commission paper submitted to the Essen Summit proposed the speeding up of trade concessions (free trade in industrial goods by 1995, steel by 1996, and textiles by 1997).

The Romanian Government is aiming for: fulfilment of the commitments undertaken by both sides in the context of association; obtaining increased assistance from the EU for the reform process and for the standards required for integration; redoubling of the efforts aimed at the approximation of domestic legislation to EU norms; inclusion in the major Trans-European Networks; and active involvement in all areas of the structured relationship. Romania would like to be involved in the preparation and proceedings of future inter-governmental conferences, and in fixing a timetable for the review of the Association Agreement and the integration of associate member states into the EU. Once EU Member States have finalised the ratification of Romania's Association Agreement, Romania's formal application to the EU could be submitted.

Romania and Bulgaria believe that it is essential that the pre-accession strategy should be applied in an undifferentiated manner to all potential candidates. Otherwise the effect would be competition among the candidates, with undesired consequences both for them and for the EU. In order to prevent the emergence of new tensions and of feelings of mistrust in the region, accession negotiations should be initiated and conducted simultaneously, albeit on an individual basis. If negotiations with certain candidates are initiated and carried out at an earlier stage, the EU should make sure that this does not happen to the detriment of the other candidates, by postponing the date of their accession to the EU.

Baltic States

The Copenhagen Council sought to strengthen trade and commercial links with Estonia, Latvia and Lithuania. The Commission has since been invited to submit proposals for developing the existing trade agreements with the Baltic States into free trade agreements. The Council has decided to sign Europe Agreements with the three Baltic States in the near future.

The Baltic States' geo-political position and small size means that they will be less of a priority in the queue to join the EU. In the interim, membership of the Baltic States raises some political and security concerns, notably concerning the treatment of ethnic minorities.

One Baltic State appears better qualified to join the EU on economic grounds than most CEECs. Estonia, by virtue of its radical market reforms, already has a well functioning market economy; it is closer to meeting the EMU convergence criteria than most CEECs.

Russian Federation

Unlike the CEECs, the Russian Federation is not yet actively seeking EU membership. Nevertheless, the development of economic co-operation with the EU is considered the most efficient way for integration into the international trading and economic system. Integrating into the European and global economies is an important means of overcoming economic crises, encouraging economic restructuring, and speeding up the transition to democracy and a market economy.

The EU and its Member States are important not only for trade; they also represent the major source of Western humanitarian and technical assistance and credit. The EU-Russia Partnership and Co-operation Agreement (PCA), concluded in June 1994, contributes to the normalisation of relations and improves substantially to the prospect for further co-operation. However, the continuation of EU protection in some 'sensitive' sectors, notably textiles and steel, and the fact that the PCA is initially non-preferential means that some discriminatory restrictions continue to apply. Even though the EU no longer regards Russia as a state trading country, but an economy in transition, co-operation is hampered by a number of discriminatory import restrictions left over from the Cold War. Nevertheless, the PCA states that in 1998 the parties will decide, in light of circumstances, when negotiations on a free trade area can start. Thus, the PCA paves the way for the economic integration of the Russian Federation into a wider European economic space.

The basic objectives of the PCA are to intensify mutually beneficial political, commercial, econonomic and cultural co-operation and to support reform in Russia. It also aims to encourage regional co-operation between the countries of the former Soviet Union in order to promote prosperity and stability of the region, and it provides a framework for political dialogue between the Russian Federation and the EU including ministerial meetings, in principle, twice a year.

The Parties are committed not to discriminate in tariff matters and they must accord each other general Most Favoured Nation (MFN) treatment as described in article 1 of the GATT. At present, Russia does not impose any quantitative restrictions on imports from the EU. However, until accession to the GATT/WTO, Russia will largely be free to increase overall tariff protection on imports from the EU. On grounds that the Russian economy is undergoing radical restructuring, it has the right to a transitional period during which it has the liberty to introduce quantitative restrictions in exceptional situations, such as sectors undergoing reconstruction; with serious social problems; where market shares face elimination, or in newly emerging sectors. Russia's scope for applying such restrictions is limited in terms of quantity and time.

The PCA contains a safeguard clause which is close to, but not identical with, GATT provisions. It allows appropriate measures to be taken when imports occur in such increased quantities and under such conditions as to cause or threaten to cause substantial injury to domestic producers. Measures to protect domestic markets can also be invoked when dumping is alleged.

The PCA aims to promote investment through provisions which envisage MFN treatment for the establishment of companies of either party in the territory of the other. It guarantees that once a company is established, it will be accorded national treatment. The Parties can, however, deviate from the principle of national treatment for companies already established in certain sectors.

The provisions on the freedom of payments will guarantee that trade in goods and services will not be hindered by exchange restrictions. Thus all payments, linked to trade in goods, services or capital, are permitted in freely convertible currency. Thus direct investment from EU companies and private persons in Russia will be freely allowed, and investors can freely repatriate their investment and profits.

The EU will open its market to Russian banks wishing to establish a subsidiary in the EU in exchange for the progressive opening of the Russian market. MFN treatment will be granted to services relating to life and non-life insurance, reinsurance, and auxiliary insurance services.

The Parties have committed themselves to remedy or remove restrictions on competition caused by enterprises or state intervention. Specifically, there should be no export aids favouring certain undertakings or the production of products other than primary products. After three years of the entry into force of the PCA, strict discipline will apply to aids which threaten to distort competition affecting trade. For the five years of the PCA's operation, Russia has the right to use aids other than export aids to support enterprises that are undergoing restructuring, or those that face serious difficulties.

Russia will endeavour to ensure that legislation will gradually be made compatible with that of the EU. Certain areas are of particular importance such as: company law, banking law, company accounts and taxes, protection of workers, financial services, competition rules, public procurement, health and safety, the environment, consumer protection, indirect taxation, technical rules and standards, nuclear laws and regulations and transport. The PCA also stresses the adequate and effective protection and enforcement of intellectual, industrial and commercial property rights.

Although the PCA goes some way towards integrating Russia into the large common economic area centred around the EU, Russia continues to be excluded from the patchwork of EU preferential trading arrangements. Such 'hub and spoke' agreements make countries outside the EU realise that anything less than full EU membership is not enough. Thus a new economic bloc threatens to again divide Europe: "the European economic area forming around the EU could develop along one of two alternative lines. One of them would leave Russia beyond the area's tariff and other boundaries while the other would . . . gradually include it . . . while finding intermediate solutions in the meantime. The former alternative would create difficulties for Russian reforms, make Russia feel mistrustful and isolated, compelled to cast about for alliances of some other kind, and increase instability on the continent. The latter alternative, however, would . . . make it easier for Russia to advance to democracy and a market economy . . . ." [4]

---

[4] Boris Pichugin, *The EC and Russia in the All-Europe Context, International Affairs* (March–April, 1994), Moscow, p. 42.

Europe has an unique chance to become a common area of stability, co-operation and prosperity. The EU as the largest single economic and trading entity on the continent must play a central role in ensuring that Russia is not isolated. As Russia cannot and should not remain outside such a bloc, possible alternatives could include: Russia's future accession to the EU; conclusion of a Europe Agreement; conclusion of a multilateral agreement on establishing a pan-European free trade area as suggested by the EU Commission in its 1992 report *Europe and the Challenge of Enlargement*; bringing forward negotiations on a possible free trade agreement between the EU and Russia from 1998 to 1995; and further bilateral negotiations with the EU, EFTA and the CEECs.

4   Economic Issues

Professor Richard Baldwin in *Towards an Integrated Europe* argued that EU enlargement to the east is unlikely for another 30 years because the CEECs are so poor, populous and agricultural that they would place unsustainable demands on the EU budget. As the V4 are two and a half times more agricultural and a third as wealthy as the EU average, Professor Baldwin calculates that, based on the EU *not* changing its policies, the accession of the V4 is not possible because it would add a net ECU 58 billion to the EU budget by 1999, a 60 per cent increase.[5] The EU's agricultural budget alone would rise from 30 billion ECUs to 45 billion ECUs, and structural funds expenditure would rise from 25 billion ECUs to 60 billion ECUs.

In the interim, Professor Baldwin proposes three options: create an 'Association of Association Agreements' (AAA) which regionalises the trade and investment liberalisation of the Europe Agreements; allow the V4 to join the EU but without the Common Agricultural Policy (CAP), EU structural aid, and labour mobility;

---

[5] see Richard Baldwin, *Towards an Integrated Europe*, Centre for Economic Policy Research, London 1994. The EU average income of $17,000 is more than twice that of the Czech Republic and six times higher than that of the poorest CEEC (Romania).

and thirdly, extend to the more advanced eastern applicants an Organisation for European Integration (OEI), essentially the EEA without provisions for the free movement of labour. Professor Baldwin's preferred immediate option would be to create an AAA, thereby rationalising the 'hub-and-spoke' bilateralism of the Europe Agreements, and then extend the single market eastwards. He believes that the CEECs should concentrate on internal reforms and increasing regional co-operation, thus preparing CEECs gradually for membership.

CEECs, who regard their accessions as urgent in order to consolidate political and economic reforms, and liberal economists believe that Professor Baldwin's economic assumptions and methodolgy are incorrect. In particular, integration is a dynamic, not a static, process. In five years time, the V4 economies are likely to have achieved a GDP around half the EU average, the same level at which Spain and Portugal joined. Such a wealth level would require a realistic rate of 4.8 growth per cent per annum in Hungary and the Czech Republic and a *slightly* ambitious rate of six per cent per annum in Poland. The precedents of Spain and Portugal indicate that the level of wealth cannot be a barrier to accession.

Professor Baldwin also failed to consider alternative budgetary options, perhaps because they are both politically difficult. Member States could increase their contributions to the EU budget or they could cut EU spending: "(the EU could) scrap the CAP, abandon the mistaken idea that poor countries need large transfers to catch up with richer ones and eliminate the overweighting of small countries in EU voting. Then the EU could be enlarged relatively expeditiously".[6]

Trade

A timetable is unlikely to provide the definitive map of how convergence takes place, however a process of elimination can help highlight the areas where attention should be given. Much

---

[6] Martin Wolf, *Why the European Union Will Enlarge Eastwards, Slowly, Financial Times*, 25 April, 1994.

trade liberalisation has already been achieved in industrial products, so little room remains for widening the scope of access. There will be free trade in industrial goods between the EU and the six associated states by 1 January 1995. The one per cent EU tariffs on steel end in 1996, and EU tariffs on associated states' textile exports end in 1997/98. This leaves contingent protection, labour mobility, agriculture, the approximation of laws, and full capital account convertibility by the CEECs as the areas where further work is needed. In addition, mutual recognition, the four freedoms and the customs union are useful areas to take forward because it would enhance integration, increase foreign investment and reduce EU reliance on anti-dumping instruments.

Market access is both the best form of assistance the EU can give economies in transition, and the most effective way of preparing CEECs for membership. The Copenhagen Council agreed to accelerate the Community's efforts to open up its markets. More balanced EU-CEEC trade could be achieved through an immediate relaxation of EU tariff and non-tariff measures; the creation of an early warning system for possible trade conflicts; elimination of subsidies for EU exports to associated countries; increased support for the process of privatisation and adjustment; greater flexibility in applying export quotas, and initiating negotiations for improved access of CEEC agricultural exports.

The EU needs to discipline itself to use commercial defence instruments only when clearly justified on economic grounds. EU states will have to develop a more transparent policy on safeguards and anti-dumping procedures (at the end of May 1994, some 19 EU anti-dumping measures were in force). Transparency and approximation of policies can help develop an early warning mechanism. A Commission paper submitted to the December 1994 Essen Summit proposed informing associate members before launching anti-dumping or safeguard clauses against cheap imports, and expressed a preference for price undertakings rather than anti-dumping duties. Continued EU application of such procedures indicates the necessity to approximate competition and state aids legislation in the CEECs.

From the point of view of associate Member States, there should be strict observance, without exceptions, of the timetable for the reduction and elimination of the quotas and tariff restrictions applied to EU exports. In this respect, the proposals contained in the EU Commission's communication *Strategy For Accession* under Section C (Enhancing Trade Opportunities), are welcome. The gradual extension of existing liberalisation within the Single Market for capital flows and trade in services to associates would have an immediate, positive effect on the volume of investments made by EU firms in the associate countries.

The Europe Agreements have 'investment-deterring effects' on assembly operations in the CEECs by setting high local content rules. In order for foreign investment to take full advantage of low labour and production costs in the CEECs, rules of origin need to be improved. The creation of a customs union would resolve any problems relating to rules of origin; moving from free trade to a customs union would not be hard for the CEECs.

CEECs need to avoid the temptation to extract from the Europe Agreements the maximum scope for new protective measures, such as under the infant industry clause. Both sides need to commit themselves to the negotiated settlement of the disputes that will inevitably arise, a task to which the Association Council machinery is well-suited.

CEECs should adopt EU competition laws and harmonise regulations in order to defuse disputes over state aids and to reduce the risk of the EU invoking anti-dumping actions. If CEECs approximated EU competition policies (in particular Articles 85 and 86 of the Treaty of Rome) controlled state aids, and adopted some of the internal market legislation with a transitional period, this would give EU business the confidence to do without, and end calls for, contingent protection. A July 1994 Commission paper proposed that each CEEC have a single authority to monitor and to control state aid, and to prepare an inventory of state aid with the Commission.

Agriculture

The Europe Agreements were least successful in liberalising agriculture. Agriculture is, and will remain, for some time the thorniest issue in EU-CEEC relations. The solution to the excess production of the CAP is to cut EU intervention prices yet further and to treat farm support as income support. However, considerable change cannot be expected until the late 1990s when the Uruguay Round cuts begin to have an impact. In the meantime, it is internal EU reform, namely the May 1992 McSharry reforms, that will reduce EU spending on agriculture. For example, in November 1994, the EU Commission announced plans to abolish 'switchover', a policy which insulates farmers' incomes from currency fluctuations, thereby saving six billion ECUs annually and reducing farm prices by 21 per cent.

Agricultural production has declined by at least 30 per cent in the six associated countries since the transition to a market economy began. Although CEECs are actually comparatively efficient producers of many foods, they have, with the exception of Hungary, become net importers of food. CEEC exports, notably livestock, slumped from a surplus in 1990 to a deficit of over 433 million ECUs in 1993.

According to a 1994 report by the Washington-based International Food Policy Research Institute, successful reforms in the CEECs and the former Soviet Union could again make these countries net food exporters, perhaps with surpluses ranging from 30 to 50 million tonnes per year. However, modernisation will be difficult. For example, nearly 30 per cent of the Polish population is employed in agriculture on small farm holdings, averaging five hectares. Modernisation would require a considerable reduction in the agricultural workforce, which is young and would add to the already high national 16 per cent unemployment rate.

If more and more EU agricultural products find their way on to the markets of traditionally agrarian CEECs, it can only be hoped that CEECs will not retaliate by adopting similar interventionist measures. However, it is unlikely that any CEEC protectionist policies will be as 'effective' as EU policies because CEEC budgets are under even greater strain and CEEC consumers are poorer.

The CAP will have to be reviewed before the CEECs join the EU. Mr. Andrzej Smietanko, Poland's agriculture minister, has stated "the same (CAP) simply can't be extended to Poland because the EU can't afford it and Poland doesn't have the resources to pay".[7] One alternative is to give half of CAP payments to the V4, however this would be politically impossible. Another alternative would be to adapt V4 production to EU norms but this would distort comparative advantage. Given these difficulties, a temptation is to exclude agriculture in order to accelerate CEEC membership, but then EU membership without the CAP is inconceivable.

Acquis Communautaire

The Europe Agreements noted that the CEECs' success in approximating the *acquis communautaire*, in particular competition and state aids, will be a determining factor in the timing of each associate's accession to the EU. Thus a cornerstone in the transition from association to accession is the drawing-up of the key elements of the *acquis communautaire* into a clear route-map or timetable. CEECs and many Member States believe that it is vital that the Commission draft a clear schedule of the essential laws and regulations for the CEECs to approximate. Without a timetable, accession will be too slow.

If the CEECs are allowed to join by 2000, they will have to approximate an estimated 200,000 pages of the EU's *acquis*, namely "the content, principles and political objectives of the Treaties, including those of the Maastricht Treaty; legislation adopted pursuant to the Treaties, and the case law of the Court of Justice; statements and resolutions adopted within the Community framework; international Agreements and Agreements concluded among themselves by the Member States relating to Community activities. The acceptance of these rights and

---

[7] quoted in Deborah Hargreaves, *Poland Calls for Radical CAP Reform, Financial Times*, 21 October 1994.

obligations by a new member may give rise to technical adjustments, and exceptionally to temporary (not permanent) derogations and transitional arrangements to be defined during the accession negotiations, but can in no way involve amendments to Community rules . . . (it may be asked) what there is left for an applicant country to negotiate with the Union . . . accession negotiations (can be regarded as) essentially concerned with obtaining . . . a seat and voice in the Council of Ministers and the other institutions, on equal terms with the existing members".[8]

Adoption of the EEA, which involved the adoption of around 60 per cent of the EU's *acquis communautaire*, made the enlargement negotiations for Austria, Finland, Norway and Sweden considerably easier. However, if a customs union and the EU's *acquis* were extended to the CEECs, this could only be a transitional phase to eventual full membership, in part because this is regulation without representation. Thus, extending the EU's *acquis* and other provisions may commit the EU to an eastern enlargement more quickly than it desires.

Economic and Monetary Union

It is premature to discuss whether CEECs can meet the Maastricht convergence criteria for full Economic and Monetary Union (EMU) because they are still in the process of transition towards adopting a market economy, their currencies are still not fully convertible, and because only two countries have, to date, submitted their applications for membership. However, it is good for CEECs to incorporate the foundations of EMU from the beginning of their economic and monetary reforms because the convergence criteria can provide valuable guidance during the reform process.

EMU requires that qualifying Member States renounce autonomy in two central areas, exchange rate policy and monetary policy. Exchange rates will be irrevocably fixed at the start, and soon afterwards national currencies will disappear and be replaced by

---

[8] Avery, *op. cit.*, pps. 29–30.

the European Currency Unit (ECU). In order to be admitted to EMU, countries have to fulfill convergence criteria relating to inflation, interest rates, exchange rate arrangements and public debt. These criteria are not absolutely fixed and there is room for political judgement, particularly on the fiscal criteria. If the indicators are outside the target range but are clearly moving in the right direction, a country can be admitted to EMU.

In EMU, monetary policy and interest rates will be managed by the European Central Bank (ECB) and they will be uniform throughout participating countries. The ECB will be European in perspective whereas the Bundesbank, which most existing European national central banks follow, is by law strictly obliged to give priority to domestic German stability.

The first stage of EMU began in July 1990 when all countries were required to lift all remaining exchange controls. The second stage, which began on 1 January 1994, involves the creation of an European Monetary Institute (EMI) which promotes the economic convergence of prospective EMU members. The third stage, featuring the irrevocable fixing of exchange rates and the substitution of national currencies by the ECU, will start in 1997 if a majority of members fulfills the convergence requirements. Otherwise, EMU is postponed to 1999 when EMU is implemented regardless of the number of Member States meeting the convergence requirements. Thus, the Treaty on European Union already formally recognises a Europe of different speeds.

In spite of the September 1992 and August 1993 setbacks for the Exchange Rate Mechanism (ERM) of the European Monetary System (EMS), EMU is not dead. The current 15 per cent wide ERM band raises the question of how to manage the transition to permanently fixed exchange rates. The Treaty on European Union states that prospective EMU members have to participate in the EMS with the normal plus/minus 2.25 per cent band. Whereas the transition to permanently fixed exchange rates in Stage Three would have been relatively easy from the latter narrow band, the problem is how Member States will make the transition from the wide 15 per cent band. Theoretically it is quite possible to use any prevailing market rate on the eve before the start of currency union. But that would be quite risky. For example, rates could be under strong market influence shortly before the final fixing or they could even be manipulated. Therefore, a start from a sustainable narrow band would be preferable.

The exchange rate crises of 1992 and 1993 provide two lessons. First, a more flexible handling of the ERM could have avoided many problems. It was wrong to treat the EMS as a fixed exchange rate regime where parities could not be adjusted any more, particularly given the large economic shock of German unification. Secondly, convergence is more important than the timetable; EMU should not begin prematurely.

Meeting the Maastricht Convergence Criteria

The Copenhagen Council said that CEEC candidates must only 'adhere to the aims' of EMU rather than specifically fulfill the convergence criteria. The differences in the level of economic development between CEEC and EU economies are so big that it cannot be assumed that they will be eliminated within the short or medium term. CEECs should aim first for balanced economic growth and then attempt to meet the EMU convergence criteria. The immediate challenge is not how to meet the convergence criteria, but how to make the transformation sustainable. Completion of the transition to a market economy is the best way to ensure that the CEECs eventually meet the EMU criteria. As there is no long-term contradiction between the criteria and transformation targets, the criteria will be useful in promoting economic reforms and growth and will improve the chances of earlier EU membership. Monetary integration is therefore an area where there is already a good road map for the accession of the CEECs.

The path towards EMU for CEEC candidates will be longer and more painful than for existing Member States, however there is no *a priori* reason why meeting the criteria should be impossible. In order to meet the convergence criteria, CEECs must lower their deficits, a goal that would be impossible without massive privatisation and reform of the public sector. Secondly, an effort should be made towards exchange rate stabilisation, however, there is the risk of serious balance of payments problems. Stabilisation is only possible if accompanied by a cautious financial policy and a suffecent capital account surplus. These policies would lower inflation, interest rates, and eventually public debt.

After joining the EU, the trade balances and current accounts of Spain and Portugal deteriorated sharply thanks to a rapid real exchange rate appreciation. As large official transfers from the EU to CEEC candidates are not likely in the short-term, every effort will have to be made to close the gap by capital account surpluses. Therefore CEECs' chances to stabilise their currencies, and to eventually meet the EMU convergence criteria, are to a large degree dependent on their attractiveness for capital exports, in particular from European countries.

In the sequencing of reforms, full convertibility must come at a later stage. Anything else would risk exposing the economy to unforeseeable events such as capital flight. Compared to the gradual removal of capital controls in Western Europe after World War Two, the international environment today is much more conducive to introducing convertibility. If the CEECs are to join EMU, their currencies must be fully convertible because there can be no currency controls in a monetary union. CEECs should gradually approach convertibility beginning with full resident current account convertibility and ending with full capital convertibility. The Czech Republic is the CEEC closest to achieving convertibility; its National Bank believes that full convertibility could be feasible within five years. However, this assumes a continued successful economic transformation and continuing internal and external monetary stabilisation.

The CEECs are far from meeting the inflation and long term interest rate criteria. Inflation rates for CEECs vary from about 20 per cent for the Czech Republic to 73 per cent in Bulgaria and 256 per cent in Romania. CEEC long-term interest rates vary from nine per cent in the Czech Republic to 68 per cent in Bulgaria and 180 per cent in Romania. It is only on current budget deficits that CEECs are close to EU levels: Bulgaria's budget deficit is about 13 per cent while the Czech Republic actually enjoys a surplus.

Among the V4 countries, the Czech Republic is considerably below the V4 average in terms of budget deficit as a per cent of GDP, inflation rate, net foreign debt as a percentage of exports, and unemployment rate. Although below the V4 average, the Slovak Republic's figures were somewhat worse, mainly due to high unemployment and the budget deficit. Hungary has the highest budget deficit and an unemployment rate above the V4 average. Nevertheless Hungary's high inflation rate is below the V4 average. Poland's figures are considerably worse than the V4 average except in the case of unemployment which is close to the average.

Simulations of the Polish economy show that it will be not be possible to fulfill all the EMU convergence criteria until 2015. While the inflation, interest rate and public debt criteria can be fulfilled in the first decade of the next century, the other criteria cannot be met until around 2015. To improve this situation, in 2000 a programme to meet the EMU criteria rapidly should become a strategic priority of Polish macro-economic policy.

Some CEECs' macro-economic policies and performance actually provide an example for some EU Member States. For example, Estonia, through radical reforms, has established a credible monetary position, notably when it effectively joined EMU overnight by pegging the Kroon to the Deutschmark. However, other eventual candidates, such as Romania, believe that the EMU criteria should be flexible. If some CEEC candidates are not offered the chance for gradual adjustment to EMU, then EMU will become an impossible obstacle that cannot be overcome.

Structural Funds

Some liberal economists believe that the EU's structural funds shelter recipients from market disciplines, retard industrial adjustment and penalise efficient producers. Other economists regard structural funds as not being well-targetted towards poverty-alleviation and adjustment in labour markets. Both groups, nevertheless, appear to regard structural funds as a threat both to the EU internal market and to the enlargement of the EU. Accession of the CEECs on the basis of the EU's current 30 billion ECU structural fund regime and the CAP is unaffordable because both new and old Member States would have to be full participants. New CEEC members would find the cost of the policies prohibitive. For existing Member States, an increase in national contributions to the EU budget to bring in CEEC members is politically out of the question. This leaves internal reform. However, reform of the structural funds is even less imminent than reform of the CAP, and the EU has decided not to review its structural funds until 1999.

Traditionally structural funds have been regarded as a compensation to poorer regions in return for the market access gained by richer areas. Currently, the EU's structural funds are allocated as follows: Objective 1 (regions whose development is lagging behind): 65 per cent; Objective 2 (conversion of areas affected by industrial decline): 12 per cent; Objectives 3 and 4 (combating long-term unemployment and occupational integration of young people): 12 per cent; Objective 5a (adjustment of agricultural structures): 6 per cent; and Objective 5b (development of rural areas): 5 per cent.

The increased cost of extending the EU's structural policies to the six associated CEECs as Member States could be more acceptable if the EU's structural funds were modernised. For example, under present practices, around one half of capital (sometimes up to 70 per cent of the cost of basic infrastructure) is given by the EU to the 'cohesion' (poor four) Member States. As areas such as transport, energy, or telecommunications are increasingly regarded as profitable investments, the EU should replace grants with EU loans, thus releasing considerable sums from the EU budget. The same rules could be applied to new members, thus saving half of the funds that would have to be contributed.

Once members of EMU, CEECs would place greater demands on structural and other funds. CEEC members would have to consider how economic shocks, such as large wage rises or a rapid oil price rise, can be absorbed in the absence of national monetary controls. EMU takes away from member states the monetary and exchange rate policy instruments necessary to alleviate shocks. Shocks may lead the country concerned to challenge ECB monetary policy and demand more transfers from the structural funds. However, EU structural funds are, and are likely to remain, small compared to national and regional programmes. This may require new policies on housing and social security that aid labour market flexibility and large flexibility on the supply side of the economy.

Another problem for new members is that investments and economic activity may be concentrated in the EU's centre where the infrastructure is best, where demand and purchasing power are above average, and from where all markets can easily be reached. Thus peripheral regions may fall behind the centre in terms of growth, employment and income. In order to attract investment, new members may have to offer substantial incentives such as subsidies and lower taxes. Peripheral countries will have to make substantial adjustments in national and regional policies.

Aid

In July 1989, the seven leading industrial nations and the EU Commission decided at the Paris summit conference to extend financial support to Poland and Hungary to help political and economic reform. The EU Commission was entrusted with co-ordinating the assistance on behalf of the 24 OECD countries. Since then, PHARE assistance has been extended to Albania, Bulgaria, the Czech Republic, Estonia, Latvia, Lithuania, Romania, Slovakia and Slovenia.

The PHARE programme is designed to support economic restructuring (especially in priority sectors such as agriculture, industry and financial services), to encourage the creation of a market economy and private enterprise, especially small and medium-size enterprises, undertake comprehensive projects, transfer know-how, and to provide technical assistance. Of particular note is the assistance being given to CEEC officials to adopt the *acquis communautaire*.

The Copenhagen Council stated that the Community should continue to devote a considerable part of budgetary resources for external action to the CEECs, in particular through the PHARE programme. The Community should also make full use of the European Investment Bank's temporary lending facility to finance Trans-European Network projects (10 to 15 per cent of PHARE's one billion ECUs in 1993 were spent on regional programmes for transportation, telecommunications, nuclear safety and environmental protection) and to relieve transport bottlenecks.

The PHARE programme has been heavily criticised, in particular by CEECs who want greater freedom to dedicate PHARE funds to infrastructure spending. The EU will need to consider carefully where the right balance lies. The PHARE programme should be revised by giving top priority to assistance for economic adjustment, mainly in the form of investment. This assistance should be gradually converted into long-term programmes for bridging economic and technological gaps between CEECs and EU Member States, similar to cohesion funds given to less advanced EU Member States. With this in mind, a Commission paper presented to the Essen Summit proposed an overhaul of PHARE including the granting of multi-annual programmes, an end to the condition that no more than 15 per cent of the PHARE budget can fund Trans-European Networks, and that aid should be guaranteed over the next five years.

5 Political Issues

Institutional Reform

An enlarged EU of more than 15 members will be unable to function unless its institutions are reformed. The June 1994 Corfu Summit made any enlargement after the accession of Austria, Finland and Sweden conditional upon success in the 1996 constitutional review of EU decision-making. The summit created a 'reflection group' to begin work in June 1995 on the "weighting of votes, the threshold for qualified majority decisions, number of members of the Commission" and other reforms "deemed necessary to facilitate the work of the institutions and guarantee their effective operation in the perspective of enlargement".

In designing institutional arrangements for an enlarged EU, there are a number of options including the present EU members plus EFTA entrants make the EU fit for an Eastern enlargement; the present EU members plus the EFTA entrants negotiate with the Eastern candidates before 1996 a partial kind of membership in specific sectors, giving the Eastern candidates an influence in intra-EU policy formation on institutional issues; the present EU members plus the EFTA entrants could ask CEEC candidates to attend the EU's own internal pre-enlargement negotiations on institutional reform in order to bind the new candidates to these changes as early as possible; and undertake an eastern enlargement without any substantial prior decisions as to institutional deepening, and leave that issue to negotiations either in parallel with, or more probably after membership treaties with Eastern candidates have been ratified. The August 1994 CDU/CSU position paper has taken the last option to be the most probable.

The first priority is to improve the legitimacy of and the possibilities for majority decisions in the Councils of the EU, and to improve the machinery of the Commission. The legitimacy of decisions in the Council will only increase if the size of population of member states is better related to the weight of their country's vote and if there is greater direct parliamentary approval of EU legislation. Either the scope for co-decision of the European Parliament with the Council and Commission is increased or, preferably, the Parliament could vote on every EU legislative act on an equal basis with the Council.

The accession of the V4 would raise the number of Council votes necessary for a Council majority from 76 to 109 and the blocking minority from 23 to 32. The share of the four large EU countries would decline from 53 per cent of Council votes to just 30 per cent, even though their collective share of an enlarged EU's population would be 56 per cent.

Suggestions for changing Council voting have included: changing the votes given to Member States; increasing the weighted vote of the more populous states and reducing that of smaller states; introducing a double majority criterion by which the qualified majority Council vote is supplemented by a requirement that a majority of the EU's population represented is also in favour of the resolution. In addition, more subjects should be submitted to majority voting in the Council.

There is also concern about the structure of the Presidency of the Council. Governments fear the constitution of weak and inexperienced troikas might harm the EU general interest. There have been suggestions to order the troikas in order to assure the presence of 'big' and old member states, and to lengthen the term of the presidency.

Changes in the Commission's role must be seen in direct correlation to its power and the expansion of the EU. The Commission could be strengthened by reducing the number of Commissioners, however this could mean that not all member states would have direct representation on the Commission. The stronger and more independent the Commission is in initiating and controlling legislative procedures, the bigger the opposition to a reduction. The more it is subjected to Council control, on the other hand, the more a reduction in the number of Commissioners appears possible.

Political Co-operation

The Europe Agreements institutionalised the forms and levels of regular political dialogue between the EU and CEECs, envisaged an exchange of information, and established further co-operation in bilateral relations and multilateral forums. For example, Article One of the Hungarian Europe Agreement states that the treaty aims to "provide appropriate frameworks between the parties toward a political dialogue which makes possible the development of close political contacts". The Copenhagen Summit sought to improve the political dialogue and to move towards a more structured political relationship. This has been partly achieved by passing from the exchange of information to political consultations.

The political dialogue envisaged in the Europe Agreements has been overtaken by the increase in the number of agreements. With six associated countries, and possibly 10 in the near future, the EU is less able to conduct so many separate dialogues. Initially too much attention was paid to the quantity rather than the quality (and results) of meetings. Too many meetings featured monologue rather than dialogue, leading to frustration on both sides. The political dialogue has therefore been increasingly multilateralised with more meetings between the EU Presidency Troika plus the six associated states, as well as between the 12 Member States and six associated states. A major example of recent 'multilateralisation' was the novel participation of the six CEEC heads of government in the concluding session of the December 1994 Essen Summit.

The CEECs want to participate fully in EU discussions, both prior to and during the 1996 IGC. CEECs want to be consulted rather than informed because they want to define their own destiny. With the participation of the CEECs in the IGC uncertain, EU Member States expect CEECs to make their views known before the IGC so that they can be taken into account by Member States. Closer involvement of the six in the machinery and substance of the EU's work is a central part of the preparation for membership. Recently this has involved participation in the meetings of the various Ministerial Councils on all issues pertaining to the JHA and the CFSP pillars. The recent Hurd-Andreatta initiative extended the JHA to the structured relationship. The September 1994 Berlin ministerial conference underlined the urgency for better co-operation between the EU and the CEECs in fighting trans-border criminality, especially in drugs, cars and plutonium.

There is common agreement that the CEECs could participate in the elaboration of EU statements, demarches and joint actions. The EU has argued that procedures could be improved by better co-ordination among CEECs. However, the CEECs are suspicious that the call for improved intra-regional co-operation is a deviation from the path to integration.

Security

The major motivation for CEECs to join the EU is security, even though most no longer fear a military threat from Russia. Membership in NATO is secondary to membership of the EU because security guarantees are already implicit in EU membership. Although the EU is not a formal military alliance, it is inconceivable that an attack on another Member State would not elicit a military response from other EU Member States.

For many CEECs, the primary motivation for membership in NATO has less to do with defence against another Russian takeover, and more to do with stabilising democracy and curtailing the potential rise of nationalist extremists. French Prime Minister Balladur's 'stability pact' used the same argument concerning EU applicants: "Central and East Europeans' eagerness for EU membership (should be used) as a lever to get them to resolve their bilateral problems. This means recognising each others' frontiers as permanent, and undertaking to treat national minorities properly".[9]

The CEECs' participation in PFP is the first step to NATO membership. PFPs intend to broaden military links in the CEECs and the former Soviet Republics, set up programmes for joint peacekeeping exercises and groom countries for NATO membership (whose membership criteria would be easier to meet than EU membership criteria). PFP countries will be able to consult individually with NATO if they believe their security is endangered. However, most NATO members have resisted formally extending to CEEC partners the benefit of Article 4 of the North Atlantic Treaty providing for automatic consultation when "the territorial integrity, political independence or security of any of the parties is threatened". Equally WEU members have been reluctant to extend the formal guarantee of Article 5, on

---

[9] Edward Mortimer, *Bigger and Better? Financial Times*, 23 November 1994, p. 26.

mutual defence, largely because of the organic link existing between the WEU and NATO. Thus PFP has not eliminated the CEECs' perceptions of insecurity.

Although NATO wishes to improve co-operation with the CEECs, at the same time it must strike a delicate balance with Russia in order to ensure that Russia is not, and does not perceive itself to be, isolated. NATO must avoid any expansion or other move which would play into the hands of ultra-nationalists in Russia or elsewhere. To alleviate Russian concerns, Russia's PFP offered a supplementary agreement which declares that NATO and Russia both have an important contribution to make to the security of Europe, and it calls for long-term co-operation, namely political consultation and the exchange of information both inside and outside their PFP. This agreement has upset CEECs who have been told that the PFPs would be non-discriminatory and would each involve the same level of co-operation.

The United States and its European partners are split over the early extension of NATO to the CEECs. Both President Yeltsin and Mr. Andrei Kozyrev, the foreign minister, warned NATO in late 1994 not to rush CEEC membership in NATO. Moscow has made it clear that it would consider an eastwards enlargement of NATO without it as a hostile act, and that the 'Cold War' could be transformed into a 'Cold Peace'. Although the Russian Federation is increasingly more relaxed about CEEC membership of the EU, an eastern enlargement of the EU could in the longer term extend NATO to the Russian border anyway because EU membership is likely to lead to WEU, hence NATO, membership.

The future nature of the European security architecture also depends upon the review of the CFSP at the 1996 IGC. There are three possible outcomes of the IGC including: building upon existing inter-governmental co-operation and continuing to rely on NATO for the provision of collective defence; setting up a European Council of defence ministers with the WEU being co-terminous with the EU, and NATO becoming a bilateral frame-work for security co-operation between the EU and the United States/Canada; and a blend of these two options.

Variable geometry already exists in the CFSP with a special regime for Denmark, different statuses in the WEU, and only some Member States participating in the Eurocorps. A variable geometry formula in an EU enlarged to the East could allow a decoupling of political and security co-operation from full economic integration as suggested in the Hurd-Andreatta proposals. Such an approach would allow the CEECs to have their say in the definition of a security policy. However, differentiation is not a panacea. The challenge will be to translate variable geometry into institutional terms.

6 Establishing a Road Map/ Timetable For Accession

The 1993 Copenhagen Summit did not set dates for eventual CEEC accessions. The June 1994 Corfu Summit stated that "the next phase of enlargement of the Union will involve Malta and Cyprus", subject to the resolution of the latter's internal conflict. Following the ratification of Austria, Finland and Sweden, the accession of Switzerland, Iceland, Liechtenstein and possibly Norway may also be likely, perhaps before the end of the century. The sequence of the CEEC accessions depends upon prior progress of reform in each country. Not all CEECs will join at the same time, and therefore there will be no single CEEC 'convoy'. Although some EU Member States believe that it is difficult to speculate which countries will be in the first group, it is *widely* believed that the Czech Republic, Hungary, Poland, Slovakia and Slovenia could join around 2000. The three Baltic States, Croatia, Romania and Bulgaria may be expected to join within the next decade. The membership of Albania, Turkey, the other former Yugoslav states, and other former Soviet Union states remains problematic and distant.

Although privately the timetable proposed by Hungary for membership by 2000 is not regarded as unreasonable, the EU and Member States have refused to elaborate an official timetable for joining the EU. However, it is known that the accession negotiations cannot begin until after the 1996 IGC. As the results of the IGC do not have to be ratified by Member States, negotiations could begin soon afterwards. However, it is impossible to know until after the IGC whether the EU will negotiate with all 12 candidates and potential candidates, or with a smaller number.

The CEECs reject the EU's view that no timetable is possible. If the CEECs cannot have a clear route map to membership, then economic adjustment and membership becomes more difficult because they will be forced to take inappropriate half-measures. A timetable should not be impossible because the EU has set targets before, such as the 1992 Single Market programe. Of the two CEEC applications received so far, both Hungary and Poland want rapid accessions with long transition periods. They believe that the Commission has time enough to evaluate their applications before the IGC; this would help them prepare the basis on which they will negotiate. Although the negotiations are likely to be difficult and time-consuming, they could be finished well before 1999, enabling Hungary and Poland to become Member States by 2000.

In order to keep enlargement 'on track', the Commission presented a medium- term strategy to the Essen Summit. This followed the Corfu Council's call for a pre-accession strategy including a White Paper listing detailed measures that the six associated CEECs need to adopt for integration into the single market, in preparation for full membership. Liberal economists have later suggested that any substantive route map should centre around the achievement of five milestones/quantitative targets: the shrinking of the state sector and growth of the private sector; the implementation of a competition policy including a reduction of state subsidies to below one per cent of GDP; a commitment to the EMU convergence criteria; the adoption of EU law; and rapid growth.

There are a number of additional factors that affect the accession timetable which are beyond the applicants' control: problems which enlargement poses for existing members; linkage with other applications, and linkage with internal developments in the EU. Experience from the EFTA accessions suggests that "it is not an exaggeration to say that the most lengthy and arduous part of the negotiations was not the Accession Conference between the Union and the applicant countries at Ministerial or Ambassadorial level, but the internal discussions of the Union itself . . . The difficulty of reaching agreement on the Union side was a function, naturally, of the fact that all decisions on common positions had to be reached by unanimity, not qualified majority".[10]

Thus the application process has its own timetable dynamic:

"each new accession . . . has militated in favour of 'grouping' (applicants), and also in favour of 1 January, which has always been the day of accession . . . There is no advantage in making a 'premature' application – on the contrary, it can lead to a long period of waiting which may politically be negative rather than positive for the applicant country . . . (however) seniority in the queue gives a certain diplomatic precedence . . . After the application for membership, the next important stage traditionally is the Commission's Opinion. Normally, the Council of Ministers requests the Opinion quite soon after the application arrives . . . To some extent, this period is a function of the complexity of the economic and political questions to be analysed . . . but it is also a function of the rapidity with which the Union wants to proceed with the application . . . The Commission's Opinion is not a legal prerequisite of opening accession negotiations . . . Probably the most significant of the different stages of the accession process is the decision by the Union to open accession negotiations, not only because such negotiations require a big input of political and human resources, but also because opening them implies a willingness to conclude them . . . the timing of the decision to conclude the negotiations depends at least as much on the applicants as on the EU . . . The final period, between the conclusion of negotiations and accession, is therefore influenced largely by the time necessary for ratification procedures".[11]

---

[10] Avery, *op. cit.*, p. 29.
[11] Avery, *op. cit.*, p. 31–32.

7   Conclusions

1.   The eastern enlargement of the CEECs following the June 1993 Copenhagen Council is no longer a question of 'if' the CEECs will join, but 'when' and 'how'. However, the date for accession remains unclear because the EU remains reluctant to commit to a date and timetable for accession. Since the EU has said that the 1996 IGC must take place before accession negotiations begin, they cannot commence before 1997 at the earliest.

2.   The eastern enlargement will be the EU's most difficult to date. While there are many obstacles, it is not in the interests of EU nations to abandon its eastern neighbours. The EU wants Central and Eastern associated states as members for reasons of economic self-interest (having access to growing emerging economies), political self-interest (enhancing democracy and stability in the CEECs), and the belief that Europe must become one again.

3.   CEECs believe Western efforts since 1989 have fallen far short of expectations and necessities. This explains why EU membership is so important for the CEECs. In spite of many declarations and promises, there is still a general lack of confidence that membership will actually happen, largely because it is perceived that the EU is looking for the least costly option.

4.   EU membership would effectively be today's equivalent of the Marshall Plan. However, the differing historical circumstances prevailing after World War Two, namely a weak world economy and the spread of Communism, may explain why the West is doing less than expected. Another explanation is that the West is still looking for progress in CEEC economic and political reforms, something that the CEECs believe can only be guaranteed by EU membership.

5.   In order to avoid the emergence of new regional tensions, some CEECs believe the accession negotiations should be initiated and conducted simultaneously with all applicant CEECs, albeit on an individual basis. If negotiations with certain candidates are

initiated and carried out at an earlier stage, the EU should make sure that this does not postpone the date of accession of other candidates.

6.   Lessons from the 1993-4 EFTA negotiations are unlikely to apply to the radically different circumstances of the CEECs. However, the negotiating procedures may be similar. The negotiations demonstrated that the accessions inevitably become bound up with the internal problems and politics of the EU. Many issues not directly linked to the negotiations have an impact on the accession process. Direct contacts between applicant countries is less important than direct contacts with Member States and the Commission.

7.   *Both* the CEECs and the EU must adjust in order for an eastern enlargement to succeed. In some areas, such as trade and the Single Market, the Europe Agreements themselves point the route the CEECs must take from association to accession. But in others, notably agriculture and structural funds, much reform in the EU is still required. An eastern enlargement is not feasible without a significant change in the way that the EU functions.

8.   While few major obstacles exist to integration on the political side, the adoption of EU laws by the CEECs, adjusting to EU standards and norms, meeting the preconditions of a fully functioning market economy, and meeting the EMU convergence criteria will be far more difficult. It is premature to discuss whether CEECs can meet the Maastricht EMU convergence criteria because they are still in the process of undertaking market reforms and their currencies are not fully convertible. Nevertheless, the best way that the CEECs can prepare themselves for EMU and membership is by speeding up their market reforms. CEECs should be judged by their economic health, rather than wealth, and their economic potential.

9.   An EU with more than 15 members will be unable to function unless its institutions and procedures are reformed. Thus a widening to the East will necessitate a deepening of institutional integration.

10. The CEECs believe that it is vital for the EU to conclude a clear timetable of the essential requirements for eventual CEEC membership. Without a clear road map to accession, CEEC membership will be impaired or even not happen. CEECs sense the urgency of elaborating a clear way forward because they fear a reversal of the reforms and successes achieved so far.

11. The eventual accession of CEECs to the EU, and possibly NATO, should not isolate the Russian Federation. While the Russian Federation is clearly far from being able to meet the criteria for EU membership, political and economic agreements must be reached in order to ensure that the Russian reform process is both encouraged and reinforced. To encompass the CEECs whilst isolating Russia would be a mistake that risks jeopardising not only the enlargement process but also the future stability and prosperity of the entire continent.

Participants:

AREGGER, Josef: Embassy of Switzerland, Warsaw
AVERY, Graham: European Commission, Brussels
AZAM-PRADEILLES, Anne: French Embassy, Warsaw
BECH, Rune: London Correspondent, *Politiken*
BERDAL, Eivind: Writer and Lecturer
BOLSHAKOV, Ivan: Ministry of Foreign Economic Relations, Moscow
BOMBIK, Svetoslav: Slovak Institute for International Studies, Bratislava
BONAR, George: International UNP Holdings Ltd, London and Warsaw
BORKOWSKI, Jan: Member of the Sejm, Warsaw
BOSTOCK, David: HM Treasury, London
BRIAN, John: GEC Marconi, Stanmore
BRÜMMER, Christoph: Ministry of Foreign Affairs, Bonn
BUDDEN, Philip: Foreign and Commonwealth Office, London
BYSTRICKY, Lubor: Ministry of Foreign Affairs, Bratislava
CUMPS, Filip: Ministry of Foreign Affairs, Brussels
CZYZEWSKI, Adam: Research Centre for Statistical & Economic Studies, RECESS, Warsaw
DEUBNER, Christian: Stiftung für Wissenschaft und Politik, Ebenhausen
ETIENNE, Philippe: Ministry of Foreign Affairs, Paris
FERNANDEZ-CASTAÑO, Emilio: Ministry of Foreign Affairs, Madrid
FICHTNER-DESSEWFFY, Eva: Austrian Chamber of Labour, Vienna
FIEDIN, Judyta: Council of Ministers, Warsaw
FOLVARSKY, Peter: Ministry of Foreign Affairs, Bratislava
GALGAU, Vasile: Ministry of Foreign Affairs, Bucharest
GALVEZ, Elizabeth: Foreign and Commonwealth Office, London
GEHRER, Silvia : Federal Ministry for Economic Affairs, Vienna
GEPFERT, Joanna: Council of Ministers, Warsaw
GIMBLETT, John: Foreign and Commonwealth Office, London
GORDON, Robert: British Embassy, Warsaw
HANSEN, Marie: Prime Minister's Office, Copenhagen
HARASIMOWICZ, Andrzej: Council of Ministers, Warsaw

HÄRKÖNEN, Aleksi: Ministry of Foreign Affairs, Helsinki
HATTINGA van 't SANT, Onno: Ministry of Foreign Affairs, The Hague
HOPKINSON, Nicholas: Wilton Park, Steyning
JAY, Michael: Foreign and Commonwealth Office, London
KALINOWSKI, Jerzy: Council of Ministers, Warsaw
KARASINSKA-FENDLER, Maria: European Institute, Lodz
KOLBRE, Priit: Ministry of Foreign Affairs, Tallinn
KOMOROWSKI, Stanislaw: Ministry of Foreign Affairs, Warsaw
KOWALCZYK, Jerzy: Ministry of Foreign Affairs, Warsaw
KRUMINS, Marcis: Latvian Parliament (Saeima), Riga
LANGHORNE, Richard: Wilton Park, Steyning
de LA SERRE, Françoise: Fondation Nationale des Sciences Politiques, Paris
LINSEN, Louise: Ministry of Foreign Affairs, The Hague
LLEWELLYN SMITH, Michael: HM Ambassador to Poland, Warsaw
LUCAS, Sylvie: Ministry of Foreign Affairs, Brussels
LUKACS, Gyorgy : Ministry of Foreign Affairs, Budapest
LYALL GRANT, Mark: Cabinet Office, London
MAYHEW, Alan: Commission of the EC, Brussels
MINTON-BEDDOES, Zanny: Economics Writer, *The Economist*, London
MURRAY, Craig: British Embassy, Warsaw
NAVIKAS, Audrius: Ministry of Foreign Affairs, Vilnius
NITSCHE, Wolfgang: Ministry of Finance, Vienna
NOWINA-KONOPKA, Piotr: Member of the Sejm, Warsaw
NYBERG, Jan: Ministry for Foreign Affairs, Stockholm
OLECHOWSKI, Andrzej: Foreign Minister, Warsaw
ORLOWSKI, Witold: The World Bank, Warsaw
OSIATYNSKI, Jerzy: Member of the Sejm, Warsaw
PATAKI, Istvan: Ministry of Foreign Affairs, Budapest
PAVLOSKIS, Olgerts: Deputy Foreign Minister, Riga
PFANN, Ursula: Ministry of Defence, Vienna
PICKING, Constanze: College of Europe, Natolin
PIETRAS, Jaroslaw: Council of Ministers, Warsaw
PITCHUGIN, Boris: Russian Academy of Sciences, Moscow
RAIG, Ivar: Member of Parliament, Tallinn

RAMSAUER, Rudolf: Federal Office for Foreign Economic Affairs, Berne
RENCKI, Georges: Commission of the European Communities, Brussels
ROLLO, Jim: Foreign and Commonwealth Office, London
ROWE, Desmond: Prime Minister's Office, Wellington
SACHS, Jeffrey: Harvard University, Cambridge, Massachusetts
SAMPOVAARA, Veijo: Ministry of Foreign Affairs, Helsinki
SARYUSZ-WOLSKI, Jacek: Council of Ministers, Warsaw
SCHIAVO, Alessandra: Ministry of Foreign Affairs, Rome
SCHMIDT, Klaus: Commission of the European Communities Delegation, Warsaw
SCHRÖDER, Ulrich: Deutsche Bank Research, Frankfurt am Main
SERDY, Andrew: Australian Embassy, Warsaw
SMITH, Alasdair: University of Sussex, Brighton
SOCHANSKA, Anna: Council of Ministers, Warsaw
STAFFANSSON, Mats: Embassy of Sweden, Warsaw
STASIAK, Marian: Council of Ministers, Warsaw
STAWARSKA, Renata: Centre for Documentation and Research on the European Union, Poznan
STEBELSKI, Stanislaw: Ministry of Foreign Affairs, Warsaw
STOW, Bill: Department of Trade and Industry, London
SUNDBÄCK, Veli: Ministry of Foreign Affairs, Helsinki
SZLAJFER, Henryk: Ministry of Foreign Affairs, Warsaw
SZUMOWSKI, Tadeusz: Embassy of Poland, London
TARNOWSKI, Pawel: Publicist; *Polityka* Magazine, Warsaw
TCHOUROV, Todor: Deputy Minister of Foreign Affairs, Sofia
TSOUKALIS, Loukas: University of Athens; College of Europe, Bruges
VAN DE WATER, Rob: European Parliament, Brussels
WALKER, James: Canadian Embassy, Warsaw
WEIGEL, Detlef: Federal Ministry of Foreign Affairs, Bonn
ZIELINSKI, Miroslaw: Council of Ministers, Warsaw

Printed in the United Kingdom for HMSO
Dd300231 1/95 C5 G3397 10170